Bruce W. Miller

HotDocs®

in One Hour for Lawyers

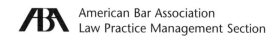
American Bar Association
Law Practice Management Section

Cover design by Gail Patejunas.

Nothing contained in this book is to be considered as the rendering of legal advice for specific cases, and readers are responsible for obtaining such advice from their own legal counsel. This book and any forms and agreements herein are intended for educational and informational purposes only.

The products and services mentioned in this publication are under or may be under trademark or service mark protection. Product and service names and terms are used throughout only in an editorial fashion, to the benefit of the product manufacturer or service provider, with no intention of infringement. Use of a product or service name or term in this publication should not be regarded as affecting the validity of any trademark or service mark.

The Section of Law Practice Management, American Bar Association, offers an educational program for lawyers in practice. Books and other materials are published in furtherance of that program. Authors and editors of publications may express their own legal interpretations and opinions, which are not necessarily those of either the American Bar Association or the Section of Law Practice Management unless adopted pursuant to the By-laws of the Association. The opinions expressed do not reflect in any way a position of the Section or the American Bar Association.

Library of Congress Catalog Card Number 98-72617
ISBN 1-57073-580-8

02 01 00 99 98   5 4 3 2 1

Discounts are available for books ordered in bulk. Special consideration is given to state bars, CLE programs, and other bar-related organizations. Inquire at Book Publishing, American Bar Association, 750 N. Lake Shore Drive, Chicago, Illinois 60611.

This book is dedicated to
Jere, Brandt, Brady, McKenzie, and Spenser
for their loving support and patient encouragement.

About the Author

Bruce W. Miller is an international corporate tax lawyer currently living in Singapore. He has been involved with document assembly for over ten years and served as an editor of the *Document Assembly and Practice Systems Report* formerly published by the Law Practice Management Section of the ABA. He has lectured on document assembly to various bar associations and published numerous articles.

Contents

Foreword

When the ABA Section of Law Practice Management introduced Gerald Robinson's *WordPerfect in One Hour for Lawyers* (DOS) in 1991, we believed that lawyers would appreciate the opportunity to learn simple word processing procedures for creating and saving documents in four 15-minute lessons. We did not anticipate the tremendous popularity of that handy little manual, which quickly became one of our all-time best-sellers, and was the flagship of software primers for lawyers that include In One Hour books on WordPerfect merge and macro functions, Microsoft Word for Windows, WordPerfect 6.1, and Quicken.

Bruce Miller's *HotDocs in One Hour for Lawyers* is our sixth volume in this series and continues our presentation of "how to" guides that go beyond simple word processing. The HotDocs program works with your word processing software to enable you to turn documents into templates that can be used as automated forms, and which prompt you for information specific to the varying needs of your clients. Mr. Miller is an international corporate tax lawyer who has been actively involved in teaching and writing about document assembly methods for over 10 years. He follows our four 15-minute lesson format to show you how to create a template in HotDocs together with WordPerfect, Microsoft Word, or Lotus AmiPro, using a power of attorney form as his working example.

In Lesson One, you will learn to start HotDocs, generate a form document using an existing HotDocs template, save the document, and exit HotDocs. In Lesson Two, you will learn how to prepare a document for automation into a HotDocs template and how to create and save a HotDocs template file from your own word processing document. Lesson Three teaches you how to customize your template to prompt you for specific variable client information and to insert the answers into the assembled form document. Lesson Four teaches you to create documents that will select among various contingencies and conditions.

For the adventuresome, Part II of the book expands on the lessons by providing instruction on how to create multiple-choice variables, compute figures and dates, create true/false values, insert text, and set up clause libraries. Mr. Miller also provides practical advice for the novice document assembler on keeping things simple and avoiding pitfalls in using HotDocs.

LPM Publishing is proud to add Bruce Miller's HotDocs book to our In One Hour series of practical software guides. We trust that you will find these clear and concise lessons in document assembly to be valuable practice tools for increasing your efficiency and providing better client service.

Robert J. Conroy
Judith L. Grubner
Co-Chairs
LPM Publishing

Preface

HotDocs is an add-on software package that works seamlessly with your Microsoft Windows-based word processor to generate legal documents. HotDocs improves the drafting process by asking the user questions about the client or transaction. Based upon the answers to those questions, HotDocs will automatically include the appropriate text and insert the answers into the legal form. HotDocs then assembles the document into a word processing file that can be edited, printed, and saved. The answers are contained in a separate file for future use.

This book is designed as a quick starter for legal professionals who want to automate their legal forms using HotDocs. The four lessons provide you with step-by-step explanations of how HotDocs can be used with your word processor to significantly improve your document production process. After completing all of the lessons, you will understand the basic features of HotDocs and how to start automating your legal forms. Beyond the lessons, several of the more advanced features are also explained, and some words of experience are given to assist you in successfully completing the automation process.

Acknowledgment

I want to acknowledge the support and efforts of Beverly Loder of the American Bar Association's Book Publishing Department in completing this book. Her encouragement and patient instructions were instrumental in bringing this book to print.

Introduction

Hardware and software you will need to get started

- HotDocs 5.0 or later (requires about 6 MB of hard disk space)
- HotDocs will run on a 386 microprocessor, but the performance will be better on a faster computer (486 or Pentium) with plenty of RAM (at least 8 MB or preferably 16 MB)
- VGA or higher-resolution color monitor
- Microsoft Windows 3.1, Windows 95, or Windows NT 3.51 and 4.0 operating system
- One of the following Windows word processors installed on your computer:
  WordPerfect for Windows (version 5.2, 6.0a, 6.1, 7.0, or 8.0)
  Microsoft Word for Windows (version 6.0, or 7.0) or Word 97
  Lotus AmiPro for Windows (version 3.0 or 3.1)

Installing HotDocs on your computer

- ▶ If you haven't already done so, install HotDocs on your computer now by following the installation instructions in HotDocs' *Using HotDocs.*
- During the installation process, you will be asked to identify the version of your word processor. If you are not sure of your word processor version number, start your word processor and look for the version number on the start-up screen. If that doesn't help, you can find the version number by clicking on **Help** and selecting **About** in your word processor.
- If your computer is connected to a local area network (LAN), you may need to have your computer personnel install HotDocs on the network before it will work properly with your word processor.

- If you are a Windows 3.1 user, after installation you should see a **HotDocs 5** program group in the **Program Manager** window. (Figure i-1).

Figure i-1 HotDocs 5 group

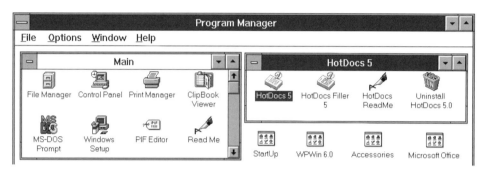

- If you are a Windows 95 user, you should see a **HotDocs 5** folder listed as one of the subfolders in the **Programs** folder when you click on the **Start** button (Figure i-2).

What you should already know

- You should understand the basics of your Windows operating system (Windows 3.1, Windows 95, or Windows NT), such as opening programs, finding files within subdirectories, and moving between open windows. You also need to be comfortable using a mouse to execute click, double-click, and click-drag-and-drop functions.
- You should also know how to perform basic tasks in your Windows word processor, such as starting the word processor, pulling down menu options, and creating, printing, and saving documents.

Figure i-2 HotDocs 5 group

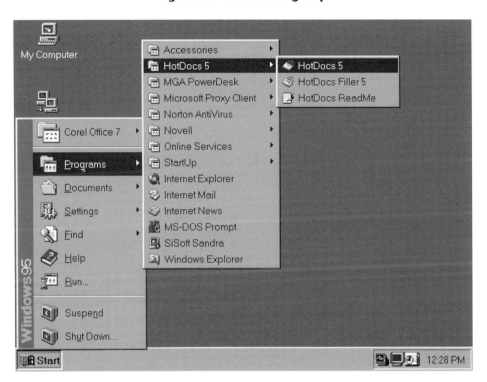

- ■ Most word processors include detailed tutorials that explain how to accomplish fundamental tasks. The tutorials are usually listed as an option under **Help.**
- ■ If you are a WordPerfect for Windows 6.1 user, you can learn basic skills in *WordPerfect 6.1 for Windows in One Hour for Lawyers,* published by the ABA Law Practice Management Section.

Conventions

▶ Bulleted text means "Follow these instructions."

Boldface italicized text is for terms first being defined.

[BRACKETED TEXT IN SMALL CAPS IS FOR KEYSTROKES.]

Text in this format is for menu options and buttons. <u>*Underlined and italicized text*</u> is text in a word processing document.

■ Text beginning with this symbol will tell you a helpful hint or an important note.

Examples used in the lessons

■ The examples in Lesson One were created with Word for Windows 6.0. For Lessons Two through Four, the examples were completed in WordPerfect for Windows 6.1. Windows 95 was the operating system used for all of the lessons.

Generating a Document from a HotDocs Template

Objectives: Learn how to start HotDocs, generate a document using an existing HotDocs template, save the new document, and exit HotDocs

The Introduction explained the things you should know before you start this lesson and verified that HotDocs was already installed on your computer. This lesson will teach you how to start HotDocs, open an existing template file, and generate a document. A template file contains the text and instructions for generating a document.

- A *template file* looks similar to a standard word processing file but has a special file name extension (i.e., **name.dot** for Word, **name.wpt** for WordPerfect, and **name.sam** for AmiPro).

You will also learn how to save the assembled document using your word processor and exit HotDocs.

Start your word processor and HotDocs

▶ Both HotDocs and your word processor must be open for HotDocs to work properly. You can start either HotDocs or your word processor first. Because you are already familiar with your word processor, start by opening it first to a blank page (Figure 1-1).

Figure 1-1   Blank Word screen

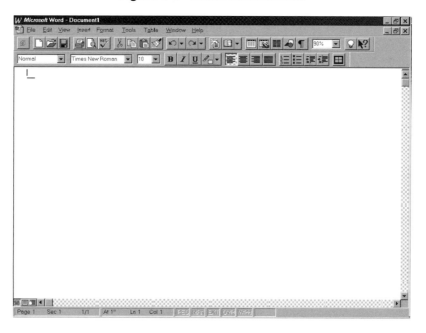

► If you installed the **HotDocs** button to your word processor's default button bar (far left button), you can start **HotDocs** by clicking on the HotDocs button with your mouse. If the **HotDocs** button was not installed, you can start HotDocs in Windows 3.1 by toggling over to **Program Manager** and clicking on the **HotDocs** icon in the **Hot-Docs** program group. Windows 95 users can start HotDocs by clicking on the **Start** button, the **Programs** folder, the **HotDocs** folder, and **HotDocs.** After HotDocs starts, the **HotDocs library** window should be displayed (Figure 1-2).

Figure 1-2 HotDocs library

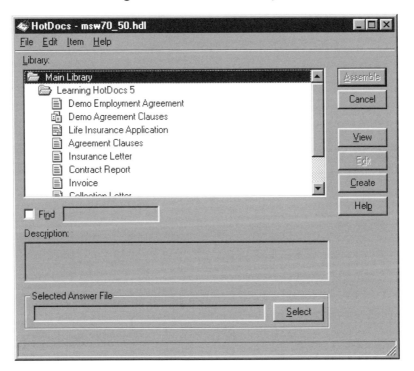

- Note that you can resize and reposition the **HotDocs library** window with your mouse to view the available folders and files more easily.

Open a HotDocs template file

The best way to understand how HotDocs works is to first assemble a document using an existing HotDocs template file. HotDocs ships with several sample template files which are listed in the **Learning HotDocs** and **ABA Tutorial** folders in the **HotDocs library** window.

▶ At the **HotDocs library** window, use the scroll bar to scroll down the list until you see the **ABA Tutorial** folder (Figure 1-3). Select the

Figure 1-3

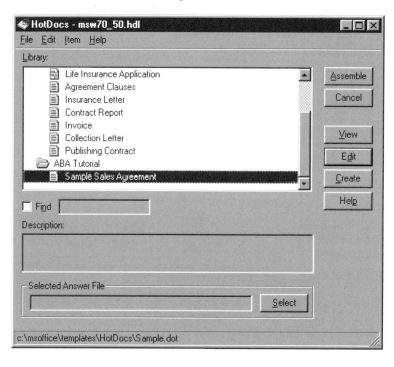

Sample Sales Agreement template by clicking on it once with your mouse. Then start the assembly process by clicking on the **Assemble** button. HotDocs will automatically switch to your word processor, open the template, and display the **Assembly Options** window (Figure 1.4).

■ The sample template file used in this lesson and the sample document used in the next lessons ship only with HotDocs 5. Prior versions of HotDocs (i.e., 1.0 to 4.1) do not have these files. You will need to upgrade to HotDocs 5 to effectively use the remainder of this book.

Figure 1-4   Assembly Options

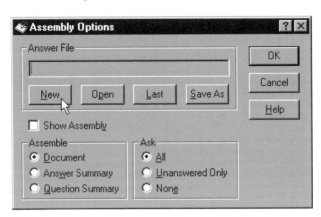

Generating a document

▶ At the **Assembly Options** window, click on the **New** and **OK** buttons to start assembling the document. HotDocs will display the first dialog, entitled **Purchaser Information** (Figure 1-5).

Figure 1-5   Purchaser Information

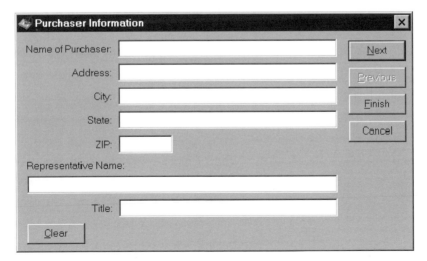

■ A *dialog* is a window that contains a group of HotDocs questions that ask for specific client information.

▶ Type MCKENZIE DEVELOPMENT CO. in the **Name of Purchaser** question box and press the [TAB] key to move to the **Address** box.

■ If you press the [ENTER] key, HotDocs will move to the next dialog window. You can back up to the first dialog by clicking on the **Previous** button.

▶ In the **Address** box, type 1502 STATE STREET and tab down to the **City** box. Finish answering each of the questions with the following answers:

City:	AMES
State:	IOWA
ZIP:	50010-0120
Representative Name:	WILLIAM B. MCKENZIE
Title:	PRESIDENT

▶ After answering all the questions, click on the **Next** button or press [ENTER] and HotDocs will display the **Land Information** dialog (Figure 1-6).

▶ In the **County Name** box, type [HARRIS], press the [TAB] key to move to the **State Name** box, and type [IOWA]. Tab down to the next box and type [THE LOT #15-230-W LOCATED AT THE INTERSECTION OF 15TH STATE STREET AND 3RD EAST, AMES, IOWA]. Note that the text automatically wrapped to the next line.

▶ Using your mouse, answer the last question by clicking **Yes** to indicate that improvements are located on the land. Click the **Next** button to move to the **Purchase Price and Earnest Money Information** dialog (Figure 1-7).

▶ Type [100,000] in the **Purchase Price** box, [60,000] in the **Purchase**

Figure 1-6   Land Information

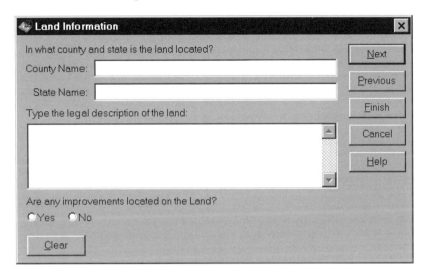

Note box, and [10,000] in the **Earnest Money** box. Click the **Next**
button to move to the last dialog, **General Agreement Information.**
▶ To answer the **Date Agreement will be Executed** question, you can
either type a date (e.g., December 19, 1997 or 12/19/97), or you

Figure 1-7   Purchase Price and Earnest Money

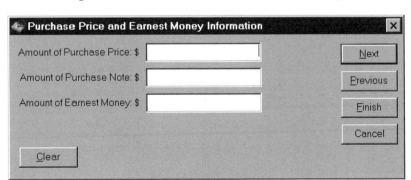

can click on the square calendar button and select a date on the pop-up calendar (Figure 1-8).

▶ Tab to the **State for Governing Law** box and type [IOWA]. Click on the **Next** button and HotDocs will assemble the sales agreement in your word processor.

■ If you did not answer all of the questions in the dialog windows, HotDocs will display a **Warning** window notifying you that the document may be invalid. The unanswered questions in the document will be enclosed with *******. Click the **OK** button to close the **Warning** window, click on the **Don't Save** button, close the word processing document without saving, and assemble the **Sample Sales Agreement** again.

Saving the assembled document and the answers

After assembling the document, HotDocs will ask whether you want to save the answers you just entered (Figure 1-9).

Figure 1-8 General Agreement/Calendar

Figure 1-9   Save Answers

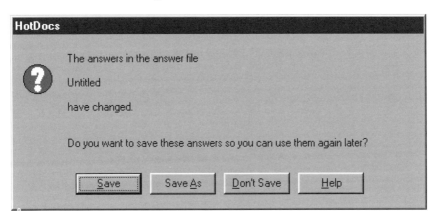

► Click on the **Save As** button and HotDocs will display the **Create Answer File** window (Figure 1-10).

► In the **Title** box, type [ANSWERS FOR LESSON ONE]. Tab down twice to the **Filename** box, type [FIRST] as the name of the new answer file, and click the **OK** button to save it.

Figure 1-10   Create Answer File

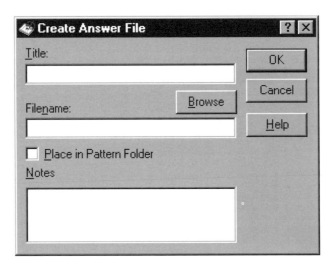

■ HotDocs stores answer files in a different subdirectory from template files. All HotDocs answer files are saved to the **\hotdocs\answers** subdirectory unless you specify otherwise. After the answer file has been saved, HotDocs displays the assembled document and automatically turns control back to the word processor (Figure 1-11). You can now edit, print, and save the assembled document as a regular word processing file.

Figure 1-11   Assembled Document

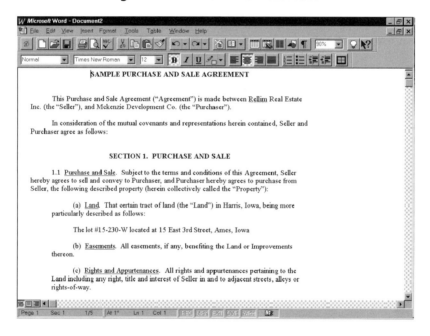

▶ If you want, you can name and save the new document in your word processor default directory. Otherwise, close the document without saving it.

Exiting HotDocs

► HotDocs remains open in the background after assembling a document. To exit HotDocs, toggle over to the HotDocs library window, use your mouse to pull down the **File** menu, and click on **Exit.**

You now know how HotDocs templates ask questions and store answers when assembling documents. Lesson Two will show you how to prepare a document and convert it into a HotDocs template.

Creating a Template from a Word Processing File

Objectives: Learn how to prepare your legal document for automation and how to create a template from a word processing file

In Lesson One you assembled a document from a HotDocs template and saw how the assembly process works. In this lesson you will learn the basic steps of preparing a legal document for automation into a HotDocs template. You will also learn how to create and save a Hot-Docs template file from a word processing file.

Document preparation basics

I.   Preparing your legal document for conversion into a HotDocs template is a three-step process. First, you should edit your forms to correct any grammar, spelling, formatting, font, or other problems. Even if you have spent many hours carefully drafting and editing your legal form documents, you will probably find at least one aspect you can improve.

II. The second step is to identify variable data within the document. *Variable data* are words or phrases that change depending upon the specific facts of the client or transaction, such as numbers, names, dates, and addresses. For many form documents, the variable data may already be identified by blank lines or brackets. If the variable data are not already identified in the document you plan to automate, you should read through the document and circle all of the variable data.

III. The third step is to identify the conditional text within the form document. *Conditional text* is included in an assembled document only if certain conditions are met. Typically, conditional text is a paragraph. However, conditional text can be as small as a phrase or as large as multiple pages. Once you have identified conditional text, you also need to identify the condition which will cause the conditional text to be included in the document.

Creating a HotDocs template from a word processing file

The easiest way to convert a legal form file into a template file is to create a template using an existing word processing file. For the remainder of this lesson and for lessons Three and Four, you will create a HotDocs template file from a sample power of attorney form document. You can repeat this same process for converting one of your form documents into a template.

▶ If you are using WordPerfect, open **power.wpd** located in the Hot-Docs template subdirectory. For Windows 3.1 users, the file may be located in the **c:\hotdocs\template** subdirectory or in another template subdirectory where HotDocs was installed. For Windows 95 users, the file may be located in the **c:\Program Files\HotDocs\Template** subdirectory, or in the subdirectory where HotDocs was installed. (Figure 2-1 shows the open template.)

■ If you are using Word or AmiPro, open **power.doc** or **power.sam**, respectively, located in the HotDocs template subdirectory. For

Figure 2-1   WP Sample Power of Attorney

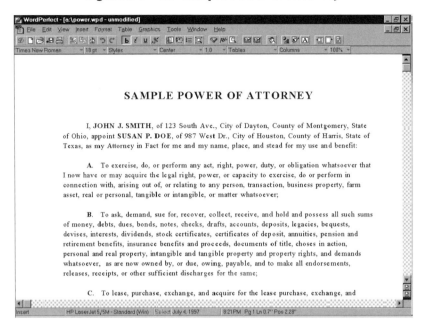

Windows 3.1 users, the file may be located in the **c:\hotdocs\template** subdirectory or in another template subdirectory where HotDocs was installed. For Windows 95 users, the file may be located in the **c:\Program Files\HotDocs\Template** subdirectory, or in the subdirectory where HotDocs was installed. (Figure 2-1 shows the open template.)

▶ Toggle over to the **HotDocs library** window and click on the **ABA Tutorial Library** folder to highlight it. This tells HotDocs that you want the new template to be stored in that folder when it is created.

▶ Click on the **Create** button and the **Create** window will appear (Figure 2-2).

▶ Tab to the **Title** box and type [SAMPLE POWER OF ATTORNEY] as the title

Figure 2-2   Create

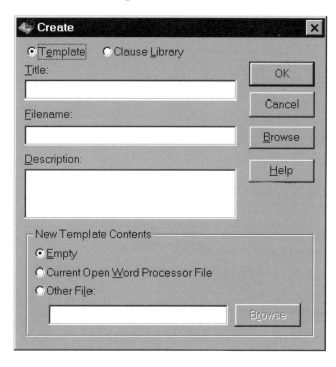

of the new template. Type [POWER] as the **Filename** and [POWER OF ATTORNEY FROM LESSON TWO] as the **Description**.

- The description is optional, but you will usually want to include a detailed description so that you can quickly find templates in your **HotDocs library.**

  ► Click on **Current Open Word Processor File** for the **New Template Contents** and click the **OK** button. HotDocs will cause the screen to jump around a few times while it creates the template. When it is finished, you should see the document text again. Notice the HotDocs button set is now displayed in your word processor (Figure 2-3).

Figure 2-3   HotDocs Button Set

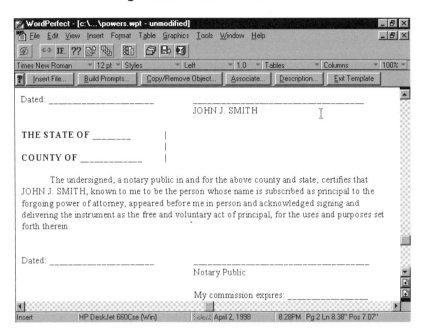

- Each button in the HotDocs *button set* performs a separate function. In your word processor, the buttons are **Variable, IF, Ask, Insert, Repeat, Test, Manager, Save,** and **Close.** In the next two lessons, we will use most of these buttons to finish automating the new template.
- Note that two files are currently open in your word processor, i.e., **power.wpd,** the original document, and **power.wpt,** the new template. For Word users, the two open files will be **power.doc,** the original document, and **power.dot,** the new template. HotDocs does not alter the original word processing document when it creates the new template.

Saving and closing the new template file

▶ To end this lesson, first save the new template by clicking on the Hot-Docs **Save** button.

■ As with using any other computer software, you will want to save your work frequently as you create and edit templates.

▶ Close the new template by clicking on the HotDocs **Close** button. The HotDocs **Close** button will also save changes you have made to the template.

■ Notice that when HotDocs closes the new template, the HotDocs button set is replaced by the default button set of your word processor. Looking for the button set is generally a quick way to determine whether you are working in HotDocs or in your word processor.

▶ You can now close the **power.wpd** document in your word processor and move to the next lesson.

You now know how to create a HotDocs template from an existing legal form. Lesson Three will show you how to identify and replace variable data in the template with HotDocs variables.

Creating and Inserting Variables

Objective: Learn how to create and insert variables into the new template and test the template file

In Lesson Two you learned how to create a template file. In this lesson you will learn how to replace the variable data in the template with HotDocs variables that you will create. A *variable* asks the user for specific client information and inserts the answer into the template when the document is assembled.

- HotDocs uses the following seven types of variables to ask for data to assemble the document:

1. **Text** - used for any type of text (e.g., addresses, names)
2. **Date** - used only for dates (e.g., 3-22-60, March 22, 1960)
3. **Number** - used only for numbers (e.g., money, salary)
4. **True/False** or **Yes/No** - used to include answers or text if the condition is met (e.g., if the answer to "Is the client married?" is yes, then spouse information will be included)
5. **Multiple Choice** - used to present a specific set of possible answers (e.g., payments made monthly, quarterly, semiannually, or annually)
6. **Computation** - used to compute an answer from other answers (e.g., if the client is male, the spouse variable is set to Wife, or Sales Price = List Price – Customer Discount)

7. **Personal Information** - used to insert basic information about you or your firm (e.g., your name, address)

- Text variables can be used to ask for any type of information because the answer can be any type of text, including numbers and dates. A number variable, on the other hand, will only accept integers, decimals, or dollar amounts.

Creating text variables

▶ Make sure that HotDocs is open. At the **HotDocs library** window, open the **Sample Power of Attorney** template you created in Lesson Two by clicking on it once with your mouse. Click on the **Edit** button and HotDocs will open the template and display the HotDocs button set in your word processor.

▶ The first variable in the first paragraph of the **Sample Power of Attorney** template is the name of the principal, *JOHN J. SMITH*. Using your mouse, select the entire name (but not the trailing comma) by clicking on the *J* in *JOHN* and dragging your mouse across to the *H* in *SMITH* (Figure 3-1).

- If your mouse skips around, you can use your keyboard instead by placing the cursor in front of the *J* in *JOHN*, pressing down on the [SHIFT] key, and using the right arrow key to highlight to the *H* in *SMITH*.

▶ With *JOHN J. SMITH* selected, click on the **Variable** button in the HotDocs button set. HotDocs will display the **Variable Type** window (Figure 3-2).

▶ Text is set as the default variable type, so you can click on the **OK** button because the principal's name will always be text. HotDocs will then display the **Text Variable to Replace** window and ask you for

Figure 3-1   Highlight of John J. Smith

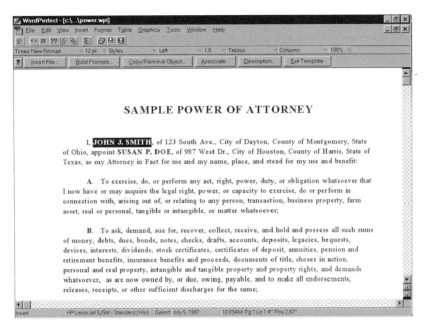

Figure 3-2   Variable Type

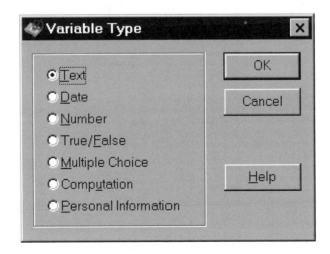

the name of the new text variable (Figure 3-3). Type [PRINCIPAL NAME] in the **Variable Name** box. Notice that **LIKE THIS** is displayed in the **Format Example** box. HotDocs automatically detected that *JOHN J. SMITH* was in all capitals and formatted this new variable in all capitals. Use your mouse to click in the **Prompt** box and type [FULL NAME:] as the prompt text.

Figure 3-3   Text Variable to Replace

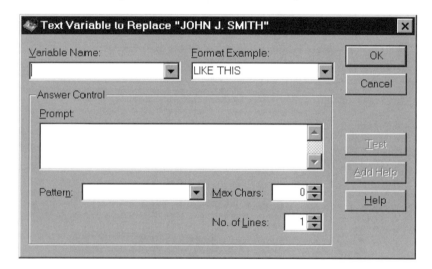

- If a text variable (such as a client's name) will appear both in all caps and regular capitalization in the same document, HotDocs allows you to change the format each place where you use the text variable in the template. As a result, you do not have to create multiple text variables (e.g., one in all caps, one in regular case, etc.).

  ▶ HotDocs allows you to test each variable as you create it. Test the **Principal Name** variable by clicking on the **Test** button now. Type in [BRENT A. BLACK] in the **Full Name** box and click on the **Result** button. HotDocs will display the result of the newly created variable. Click on the **OK** and **Cancel** buttons to return to the **Text Variable to Replace** window.

▶ To insert the new text variable into the template, click on the **OK** button. HotDocs will display a **Replace** window that will ask how you want to replace *JOHN J. SMITH* (See Figure 3-4). You can replace **All** (every place without confirmation), **Once** (the current place only), or **Confirm** (every place with confirmation). Click the **Confirm** button.

Figure 3-4   Replace

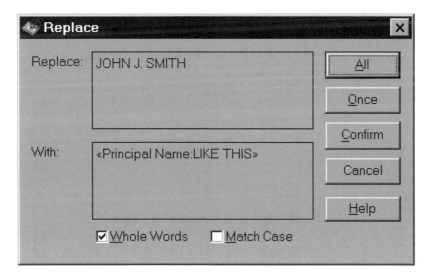

■ As a general rule, you will want to replace variables with **Confirm** to avoid inadvertently inserting a variable where one is not needed.

▶ HotDocs will replace the first *JOHN J. SMITH* after you click on the **Yes** button and search through the rest of the template for the second *JOHN J. SMITH* at the signature line. Click the **Yes** button and HotDocs will move to the third *JOHN J. SMITH* in the notary section. Click the **Yes** button to insert the variable. HotDocs will insert the

27

variable and move back to the top of the template so you can continue creating and replacing variables.

■ Notice that the new variable is enclosed in « » and that the variable name is separated from the capitalization formatting by a colon.

▶ The next step is to replace the address of the principal. Using the same method as above, highlight *123 South Ave.* (including the period but excluding the comma). Click on the **Variable** button and create another text variable by clicking the **OK** button. Name this variable [PRINCIPAL ADDRESS], type [ADDRESS:] in the **Prompt** box, and leave the **Format Example** box empty. Replace the address throughout the document with the new variable. Repeat this process for the rest of the principal's address by creating **Principal City, Principal County,** and **Principal State** text variables with respective prompts of [CITY:], [COUNTY:], and [STATE:].

▶ If you want some more practice creating text variables, you can create a similar set of variables for the Attorney in Fact, *SUSAN P. DOE.* The name for each variable would begin with [ATTORNEY] and end the same as the variables you created for the principal.

Replacing variable data with existing variables

You just created five text variables, and HotDocs automatically replaced the appropriate text with those variables wherever they appeared in the template. In some situations, you will want to insert an existing variable in another place in the template. To learn this process, you will replace the blanks in the notary section with the **Principal County** and **Principal State** variables.

▶ First, scroll down to the notary section at the bottom of the template. Then delete the blank line following *THE STATE OF,* click on the **Variable** button, and click the **OK** button. At the **Text Variable** window, click on the drop-down button at the end of the **Variable Name** box. HotDocs will list all of the text variables you have created thus far. Click on **Principal State** to select that variable, and change the formatting by clicking the drop-down button at the right of the **Format Example** box and selecting **LIKE THIS**. Then click **OK** and the **Once** button to insert the variable in place of the blank line. Use the same process to replace the blank line following *COUNTY OF* with **Principal County.**

■ If you were creating a real power of attorney template, you would want to create separate variables for the notary section in case the document was being executed in a county or state different from where the principal lives.

■ At this point, the first paragraph of the template should look like Figure 3-5.

Figure 3-5   Top of Template

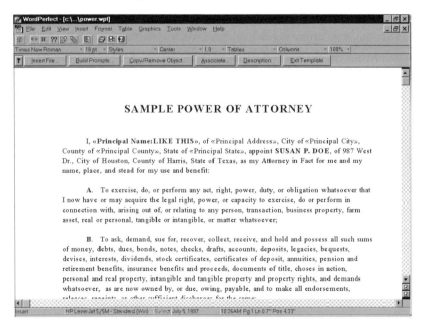

- *Helpful Hint on Naming Variables* : Use a consistent naming scheme when you create new variables, especially if you want to use answer files with multiple templates. HotDocs considers **Name of Client** to be a different variable from **Client Name.** One approach to naming variables is to only use nouns and adjectives—no articles or prepositions. This will also allow you to locate variables more easily in a list because they will be grouped together (e.g., **Client Address, Client Gender, Client Name, Client Phone,** etc.).

Creating date variables

▶ To create a date variable, scroll to paragraph I and highlight the termination date of *December 31, 1998* (excluding the period). Click on the HotDocs **Variable** button. At the **Variable Type** window, select **Date** and click on the **OK** button.

▶ At the **Date Variable to Replace** window, name the variable [TERMINATION DATE] and type [DATE OF TERMINATION:] as the **Prompt** text. If you want to change how the date is formatted, click on the **Format Example** drop-down button and select a different date format. Replace the date with the new date variable by clicking the **OK** and **Once** buttons.

Creating number variables

▶ To create a number variable, scroll down a few lines in the template and highlight *100.00* (excluding the dollar sign). Click on the **Variable** button. At the **Variable Type** window, select **Number** and click on the **OK** button.

▶ HotDocs will display a **Number Variable to Replace** window. (Figure 3-6.) Name the variable [ANNUAL COMPENSATION] and type

[ANNUAL COMPENSATION:] as the **Prompt** text. Notice that you can set minimum and maximum values for number variables. Replace the number with the new number variable.

Figure 3-6   Number Variable to Replace

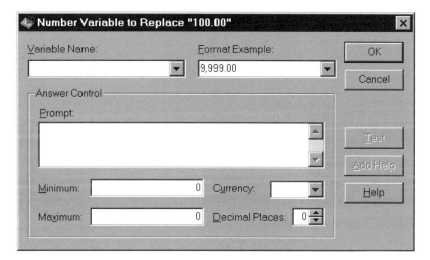

▶ You will also need to replace the written amount of the compensation. Highlight *ONE HUNDRED DOLLARS* and click on the **Variable** button. At the **Variable Type** window, select **Number** and click the **OK** button. Click on the **Variable Name** drop-down button and select **Annual Compensation**. Make sure the formatting is set to **NINE DOLLARS**. Click on the **OK** and **Once** buttons to insert the variable.

■ At this point, the bottom of your template should look like Figure 3-7.

Inserting personal information

▶ To insert personal information about you or your firm, scroll up a few lines in the template and highlight the lawyer's name, *STEVE S.*

31

Figure 3-7   Template Bottom

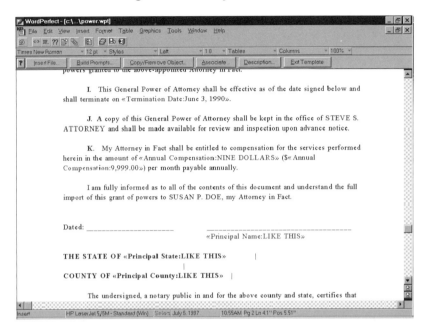

ATTORNEY. Click on the **Variable** button. At the **Variable Type** window, select **Personal Information** and click on the **OK** button. Hot-Docs will display the **Personal Information to Replace** window (Figure 3-8).

▶ In the **Personal Information** box, type [NAME] and [TAB] twice to the **Current Value** box. Type your full name in the **Current Value** box and set this variable to your name by clicking on the **Set** button. Click on the **OK** and **Once** buttons to insert the variable into the template. Notice the variable is **My Name** in the template.

■ The benefit of replacing all of your personal and firm information with personal information variables is that you can update all of your templates at one time by resetting the current value. Thus, if your telephone number or address changes, you can update your

Figure 3-8   Personal Information to Replace

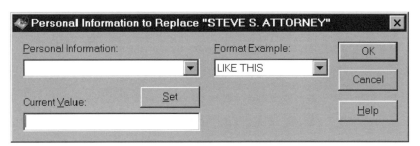

personal information in one place rather than editing all of your templates individually. This will save a significant amount of time if you use a number of templates in your practice. You can change your personal information at the **HotDocs library** window, **File, Setup** menu. Note that the changes to your personal information will be inserted only in documents which are subsequently assembled.

Testing the template while editing

■ Before testing, you generally want to save your work, so click the HotDocs **Save** button now.

▶ HotDocs allows you to test the entire template while you are editing. To test your work in this lesson, click on the **Test** button in the Hot-Docs button set. HotDocs will move to the top of the template and display the **Assembly Options** window (Figure 3-9).

▶ Start assembling a power of attorney by clicking the **OK** button. Hot-Docs will move to the first variable and display a window asking the **Principal Name** text variable because that is the first variable in the template (Figure 3-10). Notice that the title of the window is the title of the template being tested and the prompt is the **Prompt** text you entered when you created the variable. Type in a name and click on the **Next** button.

Figure 3-9   Assembly Options

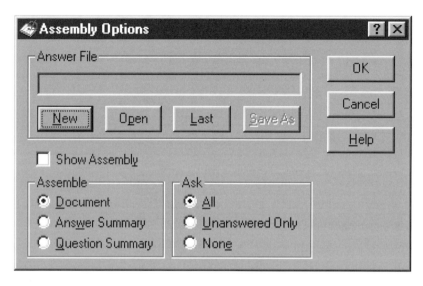

Figure 3-10   Sample Power of Attorney Principal Name

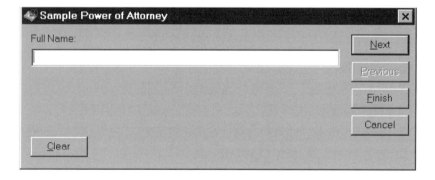

▶ HotDocs will continue to ask each variable in the template one at a time (except for Personal Information variables which are already set). Continue answering each question and HotDocs will assemble the test document. Read through the test document and verify that the answers are correct and are inserted in the right places. Also check for extra or missing spaces immediately before or after each variable. If you find an error, make a mental note of where it occurred in the test document, but don't fix it here because changes in the test document will not be reflected in the template.

■ Note that when testing a template, HotDocs assembles the document in your word processor but the HotDocs button set is still displayed. HotDocs only turns control over to your word processor when creating a document from a template—not during testing of a template.

▶ Close the test document by selecting **File, Close,** and **No** from your word processor menu bar. Once the test document is closed, Hot-Docs should display the template file again.

You now have identified and replaced all of the variable data in the template and tested it. In the next lesson, you will learn how to create custom dialogs, which will ask multiple variables in one window. You will also learn how to identify and insert conditional text.

Inserting Conditional Text and Creating Custom Dialogs

Objective: Learn how to insert conditional text commands and create custom dialogs

In lessons Two and Three, you created a new template, replaced the variable data with several variables, and tested the template. In this lesson you first will learn how to create and insert conditional text into the template. Then you will learn how to create custom dialogs.

Unlike most of the standard text of a document, ***conditional text*** is only included in the assembled document if certain conditions are met. For example, a provision identifying the name of a client's spouse and the date of marriage would only be included if the client is married. Conditional text may be a sentence, a paragraph, a section, or multiple pages. In many cases, conditional text will also contain variables. In the preceding example, a **Spouse Name** text variable and a **Marriage Date** date variable might be included in the conditional text.

Identifying conditional text

I. The first step is to identify text that will change based upon the facts of different clients or transactions. For example, in the sample template, the attorney in fact is compensated for the services performed. In some situations, the attorney in fact may not be compensated and that paragraph should not be included. Thus, that paragraph is conditioned on whether the attorney in fact will be paid.

II. The second step is to create a variable that will control whether the conditional text is included in the assembled document. To expand the usefulness of the power of attorney template, you will create a variable that will ask whether the attorney in fact will be compensated. In addition, you will need to insert an IF instruction into the template that will only include the compensation provision if the client wants the attorney in fact to be compensated.

■ An *IF instruction* is comprised of a condition and two IF statements. Similar to variables, the IF statement and END IF statement are enclosed in « ». The variable controlling the IF instruction is displayed in the IF statement. HotDocs will include the text contained between the IF and END IF statements in the assembled document only if the variable is **True** or **Yes**. If the variable is **False** or **No**, HotDocs will remove the text between the IF statements.

Creating a true/false variable and inserting an IF instruction

▶ If you are continuing directly from Lesson Three, skip to the next step. Otherwise, start your word processor and HotDocs as described in Lesson One, highlight the **Sample Power of Attorney** template, and click on the **Edit** button.

▶ In the template, scroll down to the empty line directly above the compensation provision. Including the empty line, highlight all of the text of the compensation paragraph (Figure 4-1).

Figure 4-1   Highlighted Paragraph

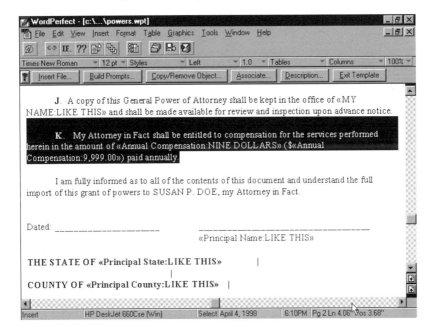

▶ To insert an IF instruction, click on the HotDocs **IF** button. HotDocs will display the **True/False Variable** window (Figure 4-2).

▶ At the **True/False Variable** window, type [ATTORNEY COMPENSATED] in the **Variable Name** box, and type [WILL THE ATTORNEY BE COMPENSATED?] in the **Prompt** box. Click on the **Yes/No on Same Line** box and then click on the **If** button. HotDocs will then (1) create a true/false variable, and (2) insert IF and END IF instructions that will include the compensation paragraph only if the user selects **Yes** in response to the question (Figure 4-3).

■ Note that you can use one variable to include multiple conditional

Figure 4-2   True/False Variable

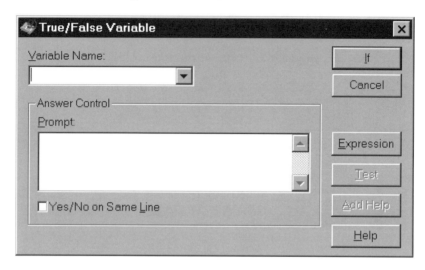

Figure 4-3   inserted IF instruction

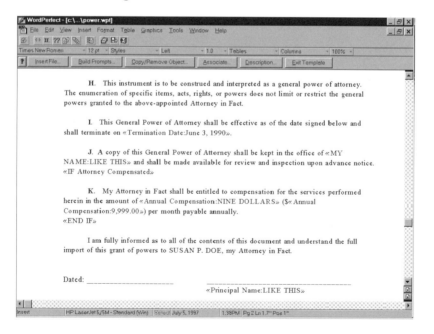

text sections in a document. For example, the true/false variable **Security Interest** in a contract template could include an entire section that describes the type of security interest and a separate sentence in the warranties section that clarifies the applicable warranties. All you need to do is insert IF instructions where appropriate and select the same true/false variable as the condition.

Creating custom dialogs

▶ When you assembled the sample agreement in Lesson One, multiple variables were grouped into three dialogs. You will now create dialogs that will organize how HotDocs asks the variables in this template. Click on the **Ask** button in the HotDocs button bar. HotDocs will display the **Dialog Builder** window (Figure 4-4).

▶ Type [PRINCIPAL INFORMATION] in the **Dialog Name** box. Notice that the listing of variables under the **Variables** box becomes active.

▶ Using your mouse, place the arrow on the **Principal Name** variable, click once, hold the mouse button down, drag the arrow over to the **Dialog Contents** box and let go of the mouse button. The **Principal Name** variable should now be displayed in the **Dialog Contents** box (Figure 4-5).

▶ Repeat the same process and add **Principal Address, Principal City, Principal County,** and **Principal State** variables to the **Dialog Contents** box. When adding new variables, point your mouse at the bottom of the list before you let go. You can change the order variables in the list by dragging and dropping. When you have finished dragging the variables over, the **Dialog Contents** box should look like Figure 4-6.

▶ Click on the **Options** button and set the **Prompt Alignment** to **Left of Field** and click the **OK** button. Click on the **Test** button to see

Figure 4-4   Dialog Builder

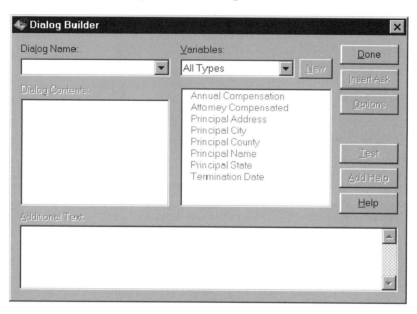

Figure 4-5   Dialog Builder 2

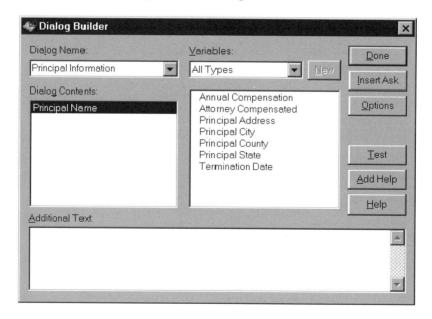

Figure 4-6   Dialog Builder-3

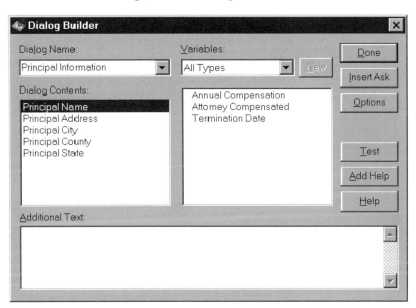

how the variables will be asked by this dialog. Note that for many dialogs, left justification may be easier for the user to fill in. The **Principal Information** dialog should look like Figure 4-7.

Figure 4-7   Principal Information

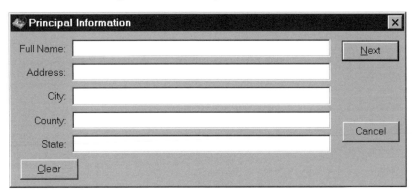

▶ Click on the **Cancel** button and HotDocs will return to the **Dialog Builder** window. Click on the **Done** button and HotDocs will return to the template.

■ If, in Lesson Three, you created variables for the **Attorney,** you should create an **Attorney Information** dialog now using the same process as above.

▶ Click on the **Ask** button again to create the final custom dialog. In the **Dialog Name** box, type [TERMINATION AND COMPENSATION]. Notice that the variables already used in the **Principal Information** dialog are marked by an *.

▶ Drag the **Termination Date** and **Attorney Compensated** variables over to the **Dialog Contents** box as shown in Figure 4-8.

Figure 4-8   Dialog Builder-4

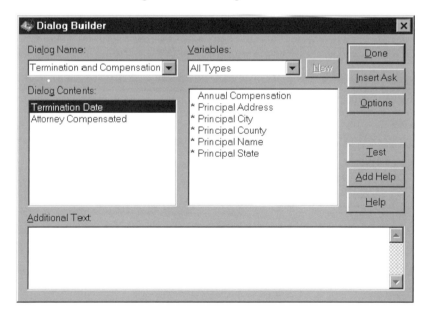

▶ When you test the new dialog, it should look like Figure 4-9.

■ Note that the **Annual Compensation** variable could not be included in the **Termination and Compensation** dialog because HotDocs would ask it even if the attorney was not compensated. Also note that you do not need to create a separate dialog for the **Annual Compensation** variable because such a dialog would only contain one variable.

▶ After testing the **Termination and Compensation** dialog, click on the **Done** button in the **Dialog Builder** window to return to the template. Save your work to this point by clicking on the **Save** button.

Figure 4-9 Termination and Compensation Dialog

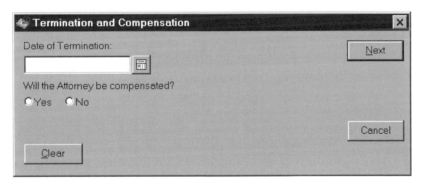

Testing and closing the template

■ Up to this point, you only tested variables and dialogs separately. You can now test the entire template to verify that the template will assemble the power of attorney correctly. First, click on the HotDocs **Test** button. Click **OK** to the **Assembly Options** dialog and HotDocs will display the **Principal Information** dialog. Type in an answer to each question, if necessary, and click on the **Next** button to move to the next dialog.

▶ At the **Termination and Compensation** dialog, enter a date for termination and select **No** in response to the compensation question. After you click on the **Next** button, HotDocs should complete assembly of the document without asking the **Annual Compensation** variable. HotDocs should also exclude the compensation paragraph from the assembled document.

▶ To verify that **IF** instructions work properly, you will want to test all conditions that affect an **IF** instruction. Therefore, you will want to test the template again and select **Yes** in response to the compensation question. HotDocs should display the **Annual Compensation** variable and should include the compensation paragraph in the assembled document.

▶ After testing the template, first use your word processor to close (without saving) all of the open word processor documents resulting from the tests. You can use the **Window** menu option to see how many documents you need to close. Then click on the HotDocs Close button to save the changes, close the template, and end the lesson.

Congratulations! In about one hour, you have learned how to create a template, create and insert variables, insert conditional text, and test the template. You can now start automating your own form documents using the basic techniques you learned in these lessons.

BEYOND THE LESSONS

This chapter briefly explains several of the more advanced features and capabilities of HotDocs and concludes with some words of experience for the new HotDocs user.

Multiple choice variables

In addition to the variables covered in lessons Three and Four, *multiple choice variables* can also be used to gather client data. Similar to a multiple choice question on an exam, a multiple choice variable asks a question and requires the user to select from two or more predefined answers. For example, Figure 5-1 is a multiple choice variable that asks about the marital status of the client:

Figure 5-1   Marital Status

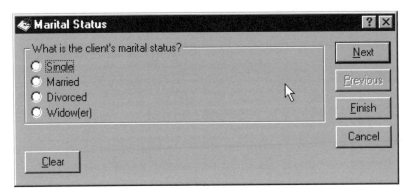

▶ To create a multiple choice variable, first highlight the text to be re-
placed, click on the HotDocs **Variable** button, select **Multiple
Choice,** and click the **OK** button. HotDocs will display the **Multiple
Choice Variable** window. You can create the marital status question
by filling in the **Variable Name, Options,** and **Prompt** as in
Figure 5-2.

Figure 5-2 Multiple Choice Variable

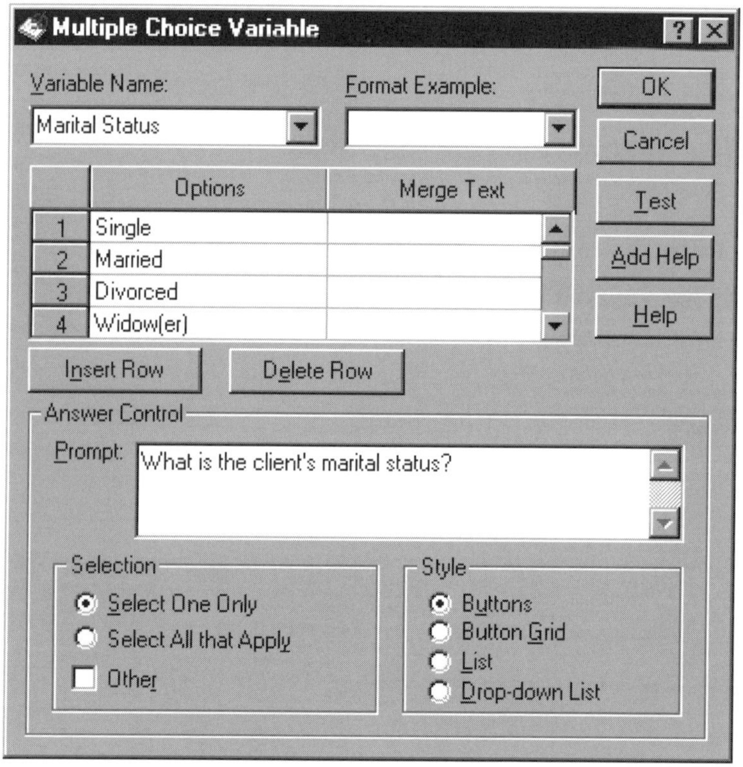

■ HotDocs displays the **Options** text in the dialog during assembly.
If the **Merge Text** column contains text, HotDocs will insert that

text into the assembled document. If the **Merge Text** column does not contain any text, HotDocs will insert the **Options** text into the document.

■ Multiple choice variables are best suited to asking for information when the applicable responses are limited to a predefined subset. In addition to presenting the user with the available options, multiple choice variables eliminate the possibility of typographical errors.

Computation variables

■ One of the more powerful features of HotDocs is that it can compute an answer or a condition based upon the answers to other variables. You can use a *computation variable* to compute numbers, dates, true/false values, or text. For example, assume you are automating a simple lease agreement that states the beginning date, ending date, and lease term. If you were to create date variables for the beginning and ending dates and a text variable for the lease term, you would need to manually calculate the ending date every time you assembled a lease agreement.

■ A better approach is to create a beginning date variable, a lease term multiple choice variable (one year, two years, etc.), and a computation variable for automatically calculating the ending date. If the **Lease Start Date** date variable and the **Lease Term** multiple choice variable already exist, the **Lease End Date** computation variable would look like Figure 5-3.

■ Using computation variables can reduce the number of questions the user is asked while assembling the document and turns over more of the mechanical details to HotDocs.

Figure 5-3 Date Computation Variable

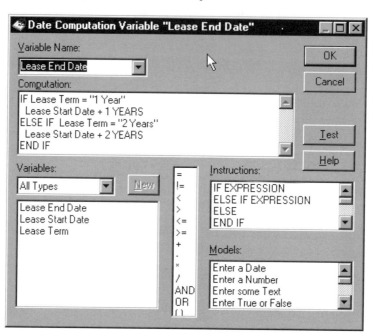

Clause libraries

■ A *clause* is a section of a document (i.e., sentence, paragraph, article, etc.) that can contain HotDocs variables. Clauses can be created and stored in a separate *clause library* folder. HotDocs also allows you to insert clauses into a template. One example of a clause library would be a real estate taxes provision library. The first taxes clause would be worded so that the seller pays all taxes. The second taxes clause would require the buyer to pay all taxes. The third taxes clause would divide the taxes between the seller and buyer via a formula. Use of clauses requires the user to identify which clauses to include in the document by selecting the appropriate clauses. Once the necessary clauses are selected, HotDocs automatically asks for any variable information contained in the clauses.

- If you decide to use clauses extensively, be sure to keep track of the variable names and use the same names consistently. As mentioned in Lesson Three, if the variable names do not match exactly, HotDocs will treat them as different variables. This will result in multiple questions for the same variable during assembly (e.g., **Name of Client** and **Client Name**), which will be confusing to the user.

- If a clause is inserted into a template, the clause will automatically appear to the user as a **Yes/No** question during document assembly. The text of the clause will only be inserted into the document if the user answers yes to the question. The text of the clause will be inserted into the document at the location where the clause was inserted.

Words of experience

Having worked through the lessons, you now have a general understanding of how HotDocs operates and how you can automate your document production. If you are like many lawyers who "discover" document assembly for the first time, you are probably very excited about automating every form you use. The following words of advice will assist you in successfully and cost-effectively integrating HotDocs into your daily practice.

1. **Start Simple.** The most important factor in successfully completing a HotDocs automation project is to start with a short, simple, frequently used form document that you can automate and quickly integrate into your practice. Even if the sole justification for purchasing HotDocs was based upon automating a large and complex docu-

ment, start by automating the cover letter or a related document first. This approach will allow you to quickly experience the entire automation process using one of your forms. In addition, you will be able to identify technical and practical integration issues before you get far down the automation path. Finally, one form successfully automated and integrated into your practice will give you the confidence to complete and the experience to properly plan the automation of larger projects. If you fail to heed these words of advice, then you might learn the hard lesson that it is infinitely better to achieve a small success than to start a monster project that never gets finished.

2. **Set Reasonable Automation Objectives.** One common mistake made by lawyers new to document assembly is to attempt to automate a complex and lengthy legal form for all possible contingencies. There are two practical problems with this all-out automation approach. First, as the number of variables increases, the number of possible outcomes increases exponentially, which frequently results in a combinatorial explosion rather than a finished template. Second, from an economic perspective, your time invested in automating those last few possible scenarios may never be recovered.

   A better approach is to set an initial target to automate your legal forms to handle 70 percent to 80 percent of the scenarios of your current and expected clients. This approach will allow you to focus on efficiently automating the main aspects of your practice and will assist you in setting cost-effective and time-efficient project plans. As you become more familiar with HotDocs and the automation process, you can always increase the scope of automating your forms to best suit your daily practice.

3. **Automate Consistently.** Just as your legal forms need to be updated and edited from time to time, you will need to periodically edit and update your HotDocs templates. You can significantly reduce your

future maintenance time by automating your forms in a consistent manner. For example, if a paragraph in the middle of a document is conditional text, you will need to include a hard return either before or after the paragraph to keep the line spacing consistent for the document when the paragraph is inserted. The approach you choose is your personal style. However, once you have decided on an approach, use it consistently when you create templates.

4. **Edit Your Legal Forms for Consistency.** Many lawyers who want to automate their legal forms have spent hundreds of hours carefully editing and thoughtfully drafting those forms. As a result, when they begin automating the forms, they do not spend any time editing or revising the form documents for consistency. Similar to the time savings mentioned above, spending some time editing your forms before you begin automating will usually save you many hours during the automation process. For example, if you are going to automate five related legal forms, you should use consistent margin settings, paragraph numbering, paragraph indenting, line spacing and signature block formatting.

5. **Select an Automation Approach.** HotDocs is a powerful and flexible document assembly program. As a result of the many features and capabilities of HotDocs, lawyers can use different approaches to automate their forms. The "master template" approach is one common approach used in automating legal forms. Under this approach, one master template will contain all of the possible scenarios of the form document. For example, a master template for a will form would contain provisions for single and married clients, clients with and without children, and life insurance or spillover trust provisions. Depending upon the specific legal form, a master template approach can result in a more complex template, which typically requires additional time to automate and test.

On the other hand, under a "related template" approach, several will templates would be created to handle the main scenarios. For example, you would create a simple will template for the single client, a married template for married clients with or without children, and a will and trust template for clients who may want to create testamentary trusts. Although this approach often is easier for lawyers to understand, maintaining and updating the related templates will require more time, because if you need to update one template, you usually will need to make the same change in each of the other templates.

6. **Know Where to Get Technical Assistance.** Even if you have a degree in computer science, you will probably run into perplexing situations when automating your forms. Capsoft has an excellent technical support staff who are patient and helpful. You can contact them at the Technical Support telephone number listed in **Technical Support** under the HotDocs **Help** menu. Capsoft also maintains a World Wide Web site at **www.capsoft.com,** where you can also get technical support, download the latest release information, or subscribe to an e-mail server dedicated to HotDocs. In addition, the Capsoft Web site lists the contact numbers for at least nine HotDocs user groups located around the United States (plus one in the United Kingdom). Finally, if you find yourself too busy to complete your automation project, the Web site lists numerous consultants who can complete the project for you, as well as published template sets you can purchase.

7. **Consider Value Billing.** Beyond the mechanical integration issues, you may want to consider value billing to maximize the economic impact HotDocs can have on your practice. HotDocs will allow you to generate legal documents for your clients in less time than if you only use a word processor. However, automating your forms and in-

tegrating HotDocs into your practice will require a capital investment of your time. As a consequence, you may want to consider billing for certain legal documents or transactions on a flat-fee basis. The ABA Section of Law Practice Management publishes two useful books on billing entitled *Win-Win Billing Strategies* and *How to Draft Bills Clients Rush to Pay*, which will assist you in implementing a billing system that economically recovers your investment.

This book has only briefly touched on a few of the powerful features of HotDocs that are important to lawyers who want to automate their practice. As with learning any new computer program, you will want to approach learning HotDocs one step at a time. Over time, your practice will become more automated and you will be able to spend more of your time on things other than the mundane and mechanical tasks of drafting documents.

Selected Books From . . .

THE LAW PRACTICE MANAGEMENT SECTION

ABA Guide to Lawyer Trust Accounts. This book deals with how lawyers should manage trust accounts to comply with ethical & statutory requirements.

ABA Guide to Professional Managers in the Law Office. This book shows how professional management can and does work. It shows lawyers how to practice more efficiently by delegating management tasks to professional managers.

Billing Innovations. This book examines how innovative fee arrangements and your approach toward billing can deeply affect the attorney-client relationship. It also explains how billing and pricing are absolutely intertwined with strategic planning, maintaining quality of services, marketing, instituting a compensation system, and firm governance.

Changing Jobs, 2nd Ed. A handbook designed to help lawyers make changes in their professional careers. Includes career planning advice from nearly 50 experts.

Compensation Plans for Law Firms, 2nd Ed. This second edition discusses the basics for a fair and simple compensation system for partners, of counsel, associates, paralegals, and staff.

Computer-Assisted Legal Research: A Guide to Successful Online Searching. Covers the fundamentals of LEXIS®-NEXIS® and WESTLAW®, including practical information such as: logging on and off; formulating your search; reviewing results; modifying a query; using special features; downloading documents.

Connecting with Your Client. Written by a psychologist, therapist, and legal consultant, this book presents communications techniques that will help ensure client cooperation and satisfaction.

Do-It-Yourself Public Relations. A hands-on guide for lawyers with public relations ideas, sample letters and forms. The book includes a diskette that includes model letters to the press that have paid off in news stories and media attention.

Finding the Right Lawyer. This guide answers the questions people should ask when searching for legal counsel. It includes a glossary of legal specialties and the ten questions you should ask a lawyer before hiring.

Flying Solo: A Survival Guide for the Solo Lawyer, 2nd ed. An updated and expanded guide to the problems and issues unique to the solo practitioner.

How to Draft Bills Clients Rush to Pay. A collection of techniques for drafting bills that project honesty, competence, fairness and value.

How to Start and Build a Law Practice, 3rd ed. Jay Foonberg's classic guide has been updated and expanded. Included are more than 10 new chapters on marketing, financing, automation, practicing from home, ethics and professional responsibility.

Visit our Web site: http//www.abanet.org/lpm/catalog

To order: Call Toll-Free 1-800-285-2221

Law Office Policy and Procedures Manual, 3rd Ed. Provides a model for law office policies and procedures. It covers law office organization, management, personnel policies, financial management, technology, and communications systems. Includes diskette.

The Lawyer's Guide to Creating Web Pages. A practical guide that clearly explains HTML, covers how to design a Web site, and introduces Web-authoring tools.

The Lawyer's Guide to the Internet. A guide to what the Internet is (and isn't), how it applies to the legal profession, and the different ways it can -- and should -- be used.

The Lawyer's Guide to Marketing on the Internet. This book talks about the pluses and minuses of marketing on the Internet, as well as how to develop an Internet marketing plan.

The Lawyer's Quick Guide to Microsoft® Internet Explorer; The Lawyer's Quick Guide to Netscape® Navigator. These two guides offer special introductory instructions on the most popular Internet browsers. Four quick and easy lessons including: Basic Navigation, Setting a Bookmark, Browsing with a Purpose, Keeping What You Find.

The Lawyer's Quick Guide to WordPerfect® 7.0/8.0 for Windows®. This easy-to-use guide offers lessons on multitasking, entering and editing text, formatting letters, creating briefs, and more. Perfect for training, this book includes a diskette with practice exercises and word templates.

Leaders' Digest: A Review of the Best Books on Leadership. This book will help you find the best books on leadership to help you achieve extraordinary and exceptional leadership skills.

Living with the Law: Strategies to Avoid Burnout and Create Balance. This multi-author book is intended to help lawyers manage stress, make the practice of law more satisfying, and improve client service.

Practicing Law Without Clients: Making a Living as a Freelance Lawyer. This book describes the freelance legal researching, writing, and consulting opportunities that are available to lawyers.

Running a Law Practice on a Shoestring. Targeted to the solo or small firm lawyer, this book offers a crash course in successful entrepreneurship. Features money-saving tips on office space, computer equipment, travel, furniture, staffing, and more.

Survival Guide for Road Warriors. A guide to using a notebook computer and combinations of equipment and technology so lawyers can be effective in their office, on the road, in the courtroom or at home.

Through the Client's Eyes. Includes an overview of client relations and sample letters, surveys, and self-assessment questions to gauge your client relations acumen.

Women Rainmakers' 101+ Best Marketing Tips. A collection of over 130 marketing tips suggested by women rainmakers throughout the country. Includes tips on image, networking, public relations, and advertising.

Order Form

Qty	Title	LPM Price	Regular Price	Total
_____	ABA Guide to Lawyer Trust Accounts (5110374)	$ 69.95	$ 79.95	$_____
_____	ABA Guide to Prof. Managers in the Law Office (5110373)	69.95	79.95	$_____
_____	Billing Innovations (5110366)	124.95	144.95	$_____
_____	Changing Jobs, 2nd Ed. (5110334)	49.95	59.95	$_____
_____	Compensation Plans for Lawyers, 2nd Ed. (5110353)	69.95	79.95	$_____
_____	Computer-Assisted Legal Research (5110388)	69.95	79.95	$_____
_____	Connecting with Your Client (5110378)	54.95	64.95	$_____
_____	Do-It-Yourself Public Relations (5110352)	69.95	79.95	$_____
_____	Finding the Right Lawyer (5110339)	19.95	19.95	$_____
_____	Flying Solo, 2nd Ed. (5110328)	59.95	69.95	$_____
_____	How to Draft Bills Clients Rush to Pay (5110344)	39.95	49.95	$_____
_____	How to Start & Build a Law Practice, 3rd Ed. (5110293)	32.95	39.95	$_____
_____	Law Office Policy & Procedures Manual (5110375)	99.95	109.95	$_____
_____	Lawyer's Guide to Creating Web Pages (5110383)	54.95	64.95	$_____
_____	Lawyer's Guide to the Internet (5110343)	24.95	29.95	$_____
_____	Lawyer's Guide to Marketing on the Internet (5110371)	54.95	64.95	$_____
_____	Lawyer's Quick Guide to Microsoft Internet® Explorer (5110392)	24.95	29.95	$_____
_____	Lawyer's Quick Guide to Netscape® Navigator (5110384)	24.95	29.95	$_____
_____	Lawyer's Quick Guide to WordPerfect® 7.0/8.0 (5110395)	34.95	39.95	$_____
_____	Leaders' Digest (5110356)	49.95	59.95	$_____
_____	Living with the Law (5110379)	59.95	69.95	$_____
_____	Practicing Law Without Clients (5110376)	49.95	59.95	$_____
_____	Running a Law Practice on a Shoestring (5110387)	39.95	49.95	$_____
_____	Survival Guide for Road Warriors (5110362)	24.95	29.95	$_____
_____	Through the Client's Eyes (5110337)	69.95	79.95	$_____
_____	Women Rainmakers' 101+ Best Marketing Tips (5110336)	14.95	19.95	$_____

*HANDLING	**TAX		
$10.00-$24.99 ... $3.95	DC residents add 5.75%	SUBTOTAL:	$_____
$25.00-$49.99 ... $4.95	IL residents add 8.75%	*HANDLING:	$_____
$50.00+ $5.95	MD residents add 5%	**TAX:	$_____
		TOTAL:	$_____

PAYMENT

☐ Check enclosed (to the ABA)   ☐ Bill Me

☐ Visa ☐ MasterCard ☐ American Express   Account Number:_____

Exp. Date:_____ Signature_____

Name_____

Firm_____

Address_____

City_____ State_____ ZIP_____

Phone number_____

Mail to: ABA Publication Orders   **Phone:**   (800) 285-2221   **Fax:** (312) 988-5568
       P.O. Box 10892
       Chicago, IL 60610-0892   **World Wide Web:** http//www.abanet.org/lpm/catalog
                    Email: abasvcctr@abanet.org

 THE SECTION OF
LAW PRACTICE
MANAGEMENT

CUSTOMER COMMENT FORM

 ABA

Title of Book: _____

We've tried to make this publication as useful, accurate, and readable as possible. Please take 5 minutes to tell us if we succeeded. Your comments and suggestions will help us improve our publications. Thank you!

1. How did you acquire this publication:

☐ by mail order   ☐ at a meeting/convention   ☐ as a gift

☐ by phone order   ☐ at a bookstore   ☐ don't know

☐ other: (describe) _____

Please rate this publication as follows:

	Excellent	Good	Fair	Poor	Not Applicable
Readability: Was the book easy to read and understand?	☐	☐	☐	☐	☐
Examples/Cases: Were they helpful, practical? Were there enough?	☐	☐	☐	☐	☐
Content: Did the book meet your expectations? Did it cover the subject adequately?	☐	☐	☐	☐	☐
Organization and clarity: Was the sequence of text logical? Was it easy to find what you wanted to know?	☐	☐	☐	☐	☐
Illustrations/forms/checklists: Were they clear and useful? Were there enough?	☐	☐	☐	☐	☐
Physical attractiveness: What did you think of the appearance of the publication (typesetting, printing, etc.)?	☐	☐	☐	☐	☐

Would you recommend this book to another attorney/administrator? ☐ Yes ☐ No

How could this publication be improved? What else would you like to see in it?

_____
_____
_____

Do you have other comments or suggestions? _____
_____

Name _____

Firm/Company _____

Address _____

City/State/Zip _____

Phone _____

Firm Size: _____ Area of specialization: _____

We appreciate your time and help.

Fold

BUSINESS REPLY MAIL
FIRST CLASS   PERMIT NO. 16471   CHICAGO, ILLINOIS

POSTAGE WILL BE PAID BY ADDRESSEE

AMERICAN BAR ASSOCIATION
PPM, 8th FLOOR
750 N. LAKE SHORE DRIVE
CHICAGO, ILLINOIS 60611–9851

Fold

AMERICAN BAR ASSOCIATION

Law Practice Management Section

Access to all these information resources and discounts – for just $3.33 a month!

Membership dues are just $40 a year – just $3.33 a month.
You probably spend more on your general business magazines and newspapers.
But they can't help you succeed in building and managing your practice
like a membership in the ABA Law Practice Management Section.
Make a small investment in success. Join today!

☑ **Yes!**   **I want to join the ABA Section of Law Practice Management Section** and gain access to information helping me add more clients, retain and expand business with current clients, and run my law practice more efficiently and competitively!

Check the dues that apply to you:

❏ $40 for ABA members   ❏ $5 for ABA Law Student Division members

Choose your method of payment:

❏ Check enclosed (make payable to American Bar Association)
❏ Bill me
❏ Charge to my: ❏ VISA®   ❏ MASTERCARD®   ❏ AMEX®

Card No.: _____   Exp. Date: _____

Signature: _____   Date: _____

ABA I.D.*: _____
(* Please note: Membership in ABA is a prerequisite to enroll in ABA Sections.)

Name: _____

Firm/Organization: _____

Address: _____

City/State/ZIP: _____

Telephone No.: _____   Fax No.: _____

Primary Email Address: _____

Get Ahead. 🏃

AMERICAN BAR ASSOCIATION   Law Practice Management Section

**Save time
by Faxing
or Phoning!**

▶ Fax your application to: (312) 988-5820
▶ Join by phone if using a credit card: (800) 285-2221 (ABA1)
▶ Email us for more information at: lpm@abanet.org
▶ Check us out on the Internet: http://www.abanet.org/lpm

750 N. LAKE SHORE DRIVE
CHICAGO, IL 60611
PHONE: (312) 988-5619
FAX: (312) 988-5820
Email: lpm@abanet.org

I understand that Section dues include a $24 basic subscription to Law Practice Management; this subscription charge is not deductible from the dues and additional subscriptions are not available at this rate. Membership dues in the American Bar Association are not deductible as charitable contributions for income tax purposes. However, such dues may be deductible as a business expense.

Membership Application